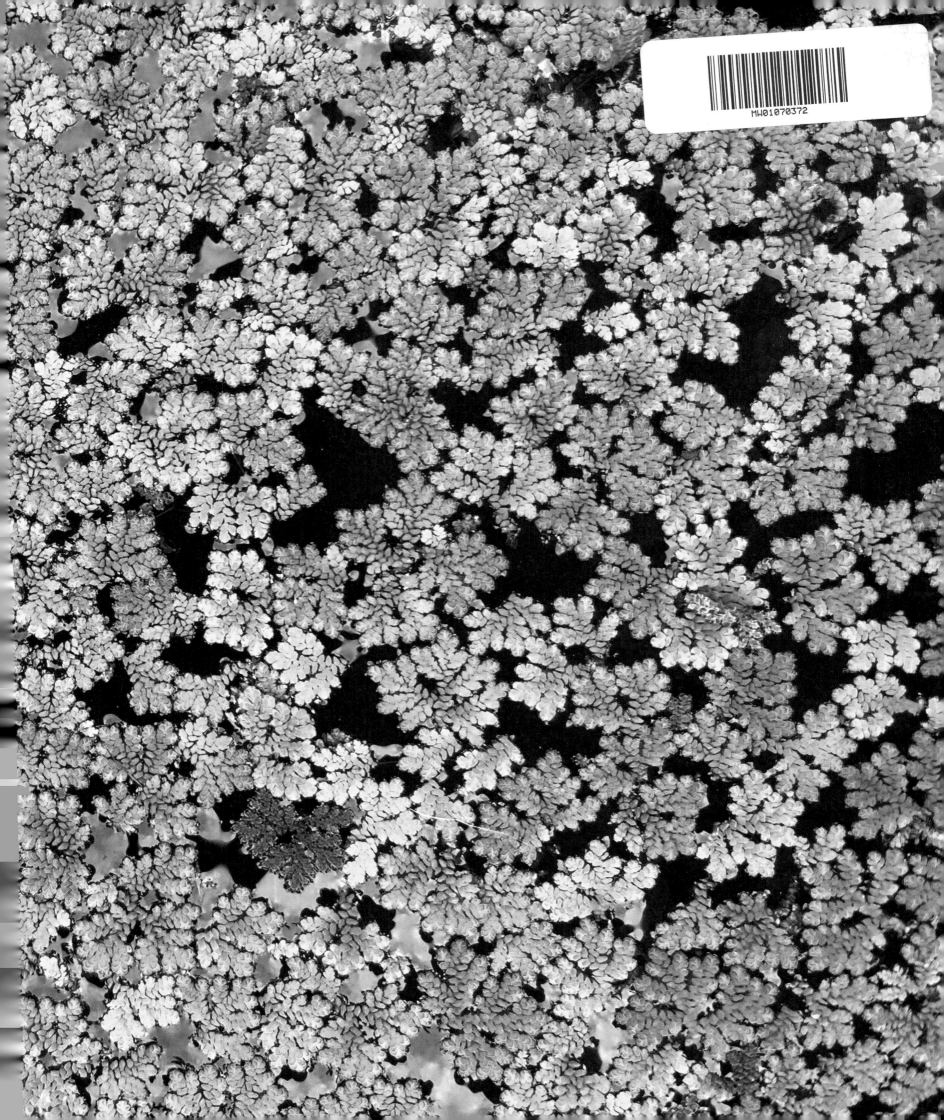

Life in the Garden

Rizzoli
NEW YORK

New York · Paris · London · Milan

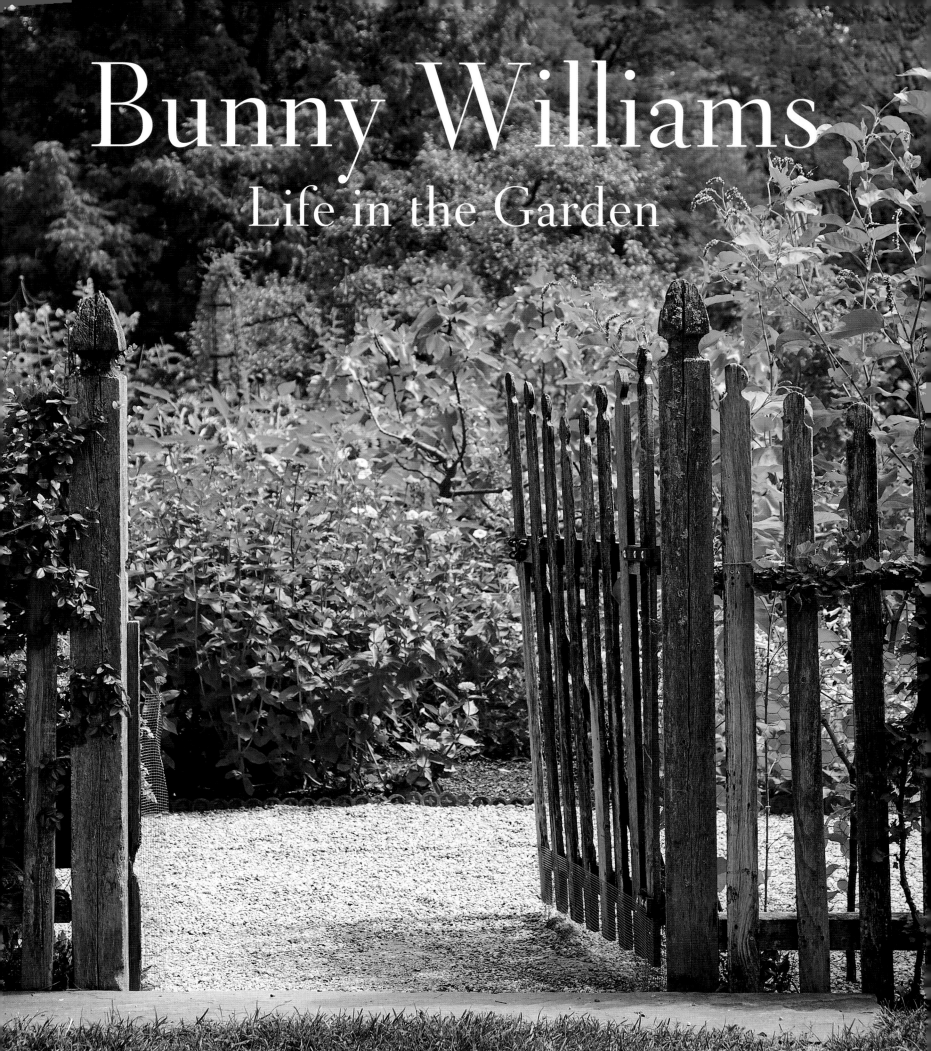

Bunny Williams
Life in the Garden

PRINCIPAL PHOTOGRAPHY BY ANNIE SCHLECHTER

Contents

Foreword 8

Why a Garden? 34

Creating a Garden 42

The Sunken Garden 90

The Parterre Garden 104

The Woodland Garden 108

The Orchard 122

The Working Garden 170

The Garden in Winter 194

Flower Arranging 242

Container Planting 250

Entertaining 282

Christmas 354

Magic-making at Aunt Bunny's
by Carter Blackwell 392

Life in the Garden 398

Resources 406

Credits 408

There is nothing more lovely in life than the union of two people whose love for one another has grown through the years, from the small acorn of passion, into a great rooted tree. —*Vita Sackville West*

FOREWORD

Sometimes, events happen in one's life that are quite unexpected. Forty years ago, when I bought this house, I had a dream of creating a home with a garden for myself and my family. Little did I envision what that garden was to become, and I wanted to share the experience of creating it with others. When Annie Schlechter, whom I had never met but knew by reputation, came to photograph our new sitting room and garden for *Veranda*, I was completely taken with her amazing photographs. I was able to see through her eyes how the property had finally matured after years of planning and hard work, and the idea for a new book came to me. Annie's eye has made it all come to life.

But this garden, and its development over time, certainly has not been my work alone. The designs and plans are mine, but I learned so much over the years about plants and their care from an amazing group of gardeners: Debbie Manson, Naomi Blumenthal, Eric Ruquist, and Bridget Lynch. But five years ago, when Robert Reimer came into our life, every part of the garden thrived under his amazing care and tutelage. The birdhouse village finally came into its own, and the floor of the woodland garden was transformed into a tapestry of color and leaf texture where every plant thrives. Tricia Van Oers, Robert's wife, nurtured the vegetable and cutting garden that now brings us not only beautiful flowers to decorate with, but also delicious vegetables for our dinners.

Once I had imagined what I wanted this book to feel like, I immediately reached out to Charles Miers at Rizzoli, who I hoped would understand my vision. He did, and his encouragement has made this book happen. Charles introduced me to Ilaria Fusina, and she, with amazing grace and patience, edited my scribbles into a coherent manuscript. And of course, we reached out to the masterful Doug Turshen to design the book. Doug and I have worked together on all my other books, but I wanted this book to be different. Thanks to Doug, Charles, and Ilaria, my dream has come true.

In addition to Annie's pictures of the grounds and our home, all the close-up images of single flowers were taken by my nephew-in-law James Gillispie. He comes over almost every morning with his wife, my niece Sarah, and while they walk their dog, Franklin, he takes pictures of what is in bloom. In fact, the cover of the book is a picture James took of clover blossoms that Sarah cut from the field and put in a basket one summer day, just because they were beautiful. This book is a family effort in numerous ways, and I was touched when my nephew, Carter, agreed to write about his memories of coming to our home over the years, as a child and, later, with his own family.

And more than anyone, I want to thank my wonderful husband, John Rosselli, who encourages me no matter what crazy idea I may have, and with whom I have the joy of sharing late afternoon walks with our dogs, stopping at each garden to take it all in and say to each other how truly lucky we are.

There is a garden in every
childhood, an enchanted place
where colors are brighter,
the air softer, and the morning
more fragrant than ever again.
—*Elizabeth Lawrence*

Here I am with my great nephew James Benjamin Gillispie,
affectionately called "Ben," and his beloved Franklin.

Why a Garden?

The longer I live the greater is my respect and affection for manure in all its forms.
—Elizabeth von Arnim

It was a daunting task to sit down with a blank pad of lined yellow paper (I always write on these, as I am more comfortable writing in longhand than typing on my computer) to start writing this book. I spent a lot of time reaching back into my memories to try to figure out where my passion for homes, and especially gardens, came from.

I grew up in Charlottesville, Virginia, on Garth Road, west of town. The road was named for the Garth family, cousins on my father's side, who had lived there for generations and had acquired a large property that spanned both sides of the road. In 1945 my parents bought a small farm and built the classic Virginia farmhouse where I grew up. When I listen to the tales of my family background, I think country life is in my DNA. Two brothers named Blackwell came from England in the 18th century; one settled in Virginia, and, from then on, the generations were landowners and farmers.

I have vivid memories of how early spring began with spreading a fresh layer of manure, produced by the local cattle, over the fields. The air was rich with a smell most people thought vile, but I rather liked its strange, sweet odor. Then the plowing would begin, and I can still see the tractors going back and forth, digging neat rows through the flat expanses of Virginia red clay soil that would soon turn bright green as the hay and corn began to sprout.

It was always amazing to see the first pink flowers of the redbuds opening, and then the beautiful dogwoods brightening the woodland landscape. Of course, I had no idea what redbuds or dogwoods were, but I was amazed by the vibrant colors that just seemed to appear when early spring arrived, as if on cue. Mommy loved going out and cutting large branches to put in vases around the house. Remembering how much I loved those trees, we added redbuds to the woodland garden here, and John gave me six dogwoods last year for a Christmas present.

On our small farm were some horses, cattle, chickens, and lots and lots of dogs (my father raised beagles). Growing up, all the food we ate came from the farm. I could not wait to get home from school, change out of my school clothes, and run outside to play with the animals, help my mother in the garden, catch tadpoles by the stream, or, when allowed, help my older brother, Jimmy, build a fort in the woods.

In one of the fields on the property there were some giant ancient apple trees, and as the spring sun warmed the soil, thousands of daffodils appeared around them. I could already smell them as I ran out to cut a bouquet of the golden yellow blossoms for my mother. They must have been planted many years before my parents bought the property, as the bulbs had spread to make what seemed like a gigantic yellow carpet. There was a brick walk to the front door of the house lined with boxwood and two large southern magnolia trees. My mother would cut the magnolias and boxwood to make Christmas wreaths for the house and the annual Christmas church bazaar, and she let me help her.

Along the south side of the house was an open porch where Mommy had trained morning glories on a trellis to block out the hard afternoon sun. I loved going out in the morning to see them all in bloom for a few hours. It made me sad when they closed for the day, but I knew they would open again, to my delight, the next day. In the early summer mornings, I would gather eggs from the chicken house and help my mother and

Mrs. McAllister, who lived on the property, in the vegetable garden. As I loved digging in the dirt, we made holes for squash seeds and, later in the summer, reveled at the large gourds attached to the long vines. Helping to pick peas and tomatoes off the vine was another chore I loved. Afterward I would watch mother and Mrs. McAllister make sauces and jams and prepare vegetables for the large freezer on the back porch.

One of my favorite places to run to was Mrs. McAllister's house, across the field. The most delicious scents emanated from her wood-burning stove, and she would sit me at her large kitchen table covered with red-and-white checked oilcloth. Homemade jams and apple butter were in mason jars in the center, and she would serve me one of her homemade biscuits, fresh from the oven and smothered in her hand-churned butter and various fruit jams, with a cold glass of fresh milk or a cup of mint tea. When I think back to those times, I realize that this is where my passion for the vegetable garden and the desire to have an orchard with apples, pears, and cherries came from. Now I try and re-create the savories and chutneys I so loved as a child.

Often at the end of the day, I would sit on the back terrace with my parents, my brother, and sometimes their friends while they had a cocktail before dinner. We would all watch the sun set over the lawn and the fields, with the beautiful Blue Ridge Mountains in the distance. Although you don't know it at the time, those experiences are the makings of your memories, so when I first came to the northwest corner of Connecticut years later, seeing the distant hills of the Berkshires and the vast fields filled with grazing cows, I knew I had found the place I wanted to have a home, as it so reminded me of my native Virginia.

The house as I found it and an early family gathering. Clockwise from left: my nephew Carter, John, my brother Jimmy, niece Sarah, sister-in-law Margaret, and myself with three Norfolk terriers.

CREATING A GARDEN

A garden is like those pernicious machineries which catch a man's coat-skirt or his hand, and draw in his arm, his leg, and his whole body to irresistible destruction. —Ralph Waldo Emerson

After college, I wanted more than anything to move to New York City to pursue a career in interior design, a dream that I had in the back of my mind since I was a teenager. Living in the city was exciting and stimulating for the first few years, but when I married in my late twenties, I longed for a small place in the country because I missed the open space and the feeling of being a part of nature. We were very lucky to be able to rent an 18th-century farmhouse on a big piece of property in Massachusetts, just over the Connecticut border, where I planted vegetables and created my first cutting garden. We lived there for several years, but as I became more serious about gardening, I realized that I should do it on property we owned. Thus began the hunt for a permanent home.

For two years we searched and searched, and it wasn't until I turned into the driveway of Brewster Road that I found what I'd been looking for. Whether it was the large allée of mature locust trees that lined the driveway ending at a huge catalpa tree, or the two imposing sugar maples that flanked the white house sitting on a slight knoll, it was love at first sight and, as such, I saw no faults. Little did I know—or want to know—what upkeep these magnificent old trees would require, or that some presented hazards that would necessitate their removal at a significant cost to our limited funds. But eager as I was to start planting, tree maintenance was the first order of business.

As a fledgling interior designer, I arrogantly thought that designing a garden for myself would be easy. I had to take a step back and become a student again, and although I made—and corrected—many mistakes over the years, the process was never dull. One thing I learned is that it's just as well that I didn't have a clear plan at the outset, because nature had a plan of its own.

Since I was in a hurry at first, I began with a flat, sunny spot on the south side of the house. This area, formerly a lawn tennis court (I learned this from older villagers who had been guests in the house formerly owned by Mr. and Mrs. Knowlton), provided a lovely view from the screened porch.

As there were two large crabapples along the south border with a scrubby hedge on each side, I immediately envisioned my first garden "room," but it would need some structure. The land also sloped into the space, so I felt it should be terraced with gracious steps. Our dear friend the artist Christopher Hewat, who grew up nearby and had a passion for the stone walls you see all over the countryside in northwestern Connecticut, built a wall along the north edge for us. On each end I had tall lattice fences built to form the back wall of the perennial border and to create a doorway to the area beyond. I designed a rounded arch to be placed between the two crabapples, and in front of the lattices I dug two forty-foot-long, five-foot-deep beds so I could begin planting. I filled the beds with some of my favorite flowers: peonies, roses, foxgloves, lilies, and lavender. Each weekend I rushed to our house in the country to weed, water, deadhead, and see what was in bloom. As I had no planting plan per se, I often bought whatever looked good in the nursery. The joy was in the process, but as the summer went on, I found that my beds were not fabulous—height and color were wrong, and textures were not complementary. That is when I realized I needed to educate myself. With the help of my wonderful bookdealer friends Timothy Mawson and Mike

McCabe, I started a gardening library and spent my evenings devouring the writing of Vita Sackville-West, Gertrude Jekyll, Christopher Lloyd, and Russell Page, to name a few. I also knew that even though I had visited many American gardens with my mother when I was young, I needed to travel and see other gardens. My first trip to England was like searching for the holy grail. Walking through the gardens at Sissinghurst and Hidcote for the first time was exhilarating.

It was while touring Sissinghurst that I really began to understand the importance of a plan that would create a "room" for each garden space. At Sissinghurst, one garden room leads to another, just as rooms in a house are connected by halls. After each visit, I returned home to rethink my own garden. I moved on from the sunken garden to relocate the vegetable garden so it would connect to the original barn on the property. We enclosed the spaces by adding a board fence along the three sides and crafting a rustic arbor of oak branches on the end to grow trailing roses and clematis. I eventually added a hornbeam hedge on the north side to enclose the space even more. Because this was where my compost pile had been, it became a very rich planting area.

Years later, I found an amazing set of 19th-century windows and used them to replace a tiny greenhouse that was attached to the barn to create the "conservatory." It wasn't until John decided that we should renovate the barn (we turned it into a large space for entertaining and created a guestroom in the old hayloft) that the conservatory became an additional dining room. At this point we had to build another working barn to hold all the gardening equipment we had accumulated, so I began to develop the area I call the "working garden." I added a large greenhouse on the north side of a new larger vegetable and cutting garden, and nearby I built a chicken pavilion consisting of two henhouses connected to an octagonal cage in the center. Since the old vegetable garden outside of the conservatory needed a redo, I decided to

create a parterre garden within the original space. Small boxwoods were laid out in geometric shapes for the early spring, and annuals for the summer.

Eventually I was able to buy an adjacent piece of property that became a fruit orchard with apple, pear, and cherry trees. Later I created a path to our pool, which I placed on a high knoll to have a view of the hillside beyond. When John and I were shopping in the South of France for our store, Treillage (now closed), we came upon a large set of coping stones from a 19th-century basin that John immediately said should become our pool. When we chose this site for the pool, we also needed a pool house with a powder room, a small kitchen, and a large open space to sit in the shade. One day, the design for the pool house just came to me. The nearby town of Falls Village is filled with Greek Revival architecture, and it dawned on me that it should look as though out of the woods a great temple had emerged.

Each year I planned a garden trip to another country, and wherever I traveled, I visited the local botanical gardens and attended countless lectures by garden experts and designers, all in the hope of educating myself. The Elizabethan gardens at Hatfield House, the hedge garden rooms at Hidcote, and the parklike gardens at Rousham, Great Dixter, and Iford Manor are just a few of the places that have influenced me. It was in Italy that I saw the beautiful garden ornaments that punctuated the more-architectural designs favored there and where I fell in love with the cypress tree. Since the cypress cannot grow in Connecticut, I've used arborvitae in its place for an "Italian moment." The potagers in France blew me away with their plantings of vegetables and herbs creating beautiful rhythms of pattern, color, and texture. However, as much as I loved the wall tiles of Portuguese gardens, I knew they had no place in my Connecticut garden, so I refrained from painting all my pots in the fabulous blue that I had seen at the Majorelle Gardens in Marrakech.

sunset muskmallow
Abelmoschus manihot
'Cream Cup'

Blue-Eyed Susan passionflower
Passiflora 'Blue Eyed Susan'
(Passiflora incarnata x P. edulis) x
(P. incarnata x P. cincinnata)

bear's breeches
Acanthus hungaricus

'Hartlage Wine'
Carolina allspice
Calycanthus x *raulstonii*
'Hartlage Wine'

fountain grass
Pennisetum alopecuroides
'Hameln'

Red Heart Rose of Sharon
Hibiscus syriacus L. 'Red Heart'

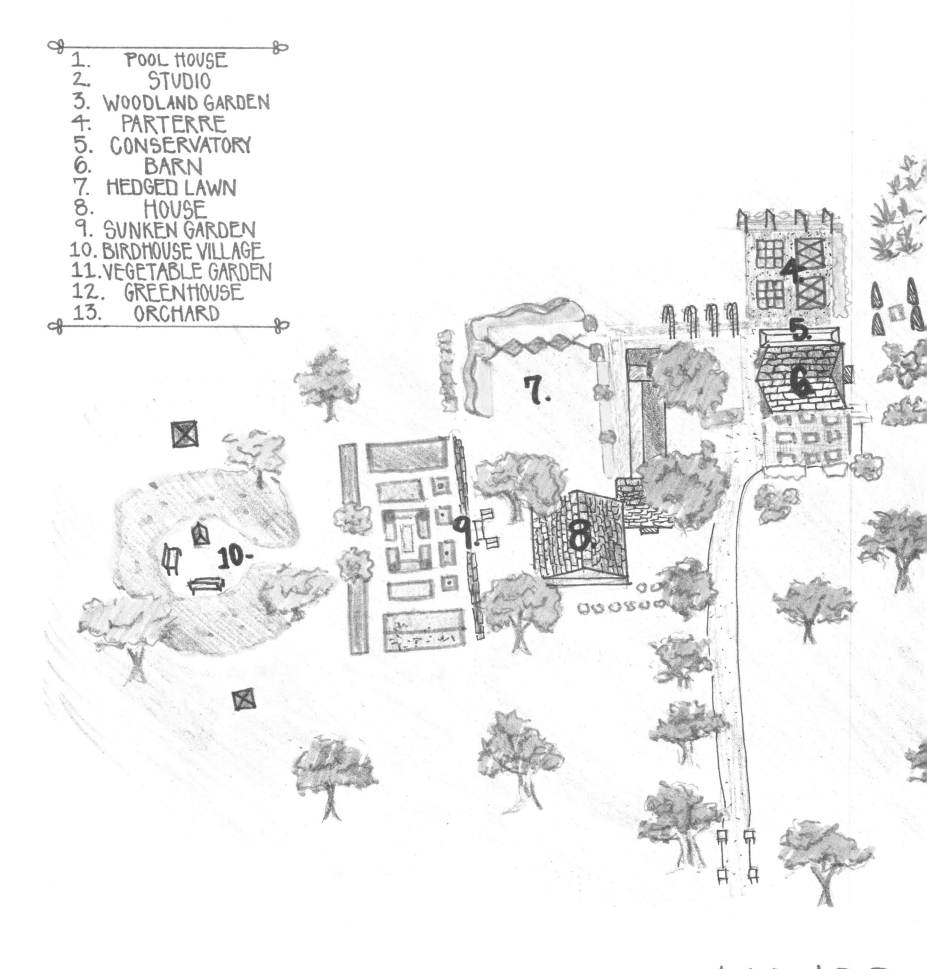

1.   POOL HOUSE
2.   STUDIO
3. WOODLAND GARDEN
4.   PARTERRE
5.   CONSERVATORY
6.   BARN
7.   HEDGED LAWN
8.   HOUSE
9.   SUNKEN GARDEN
10. BIRDHOUSE VILLAGE
11. VEGETABLE GARDEN
12.   GREENHOUSE
13.   ORCHARD

MANOR

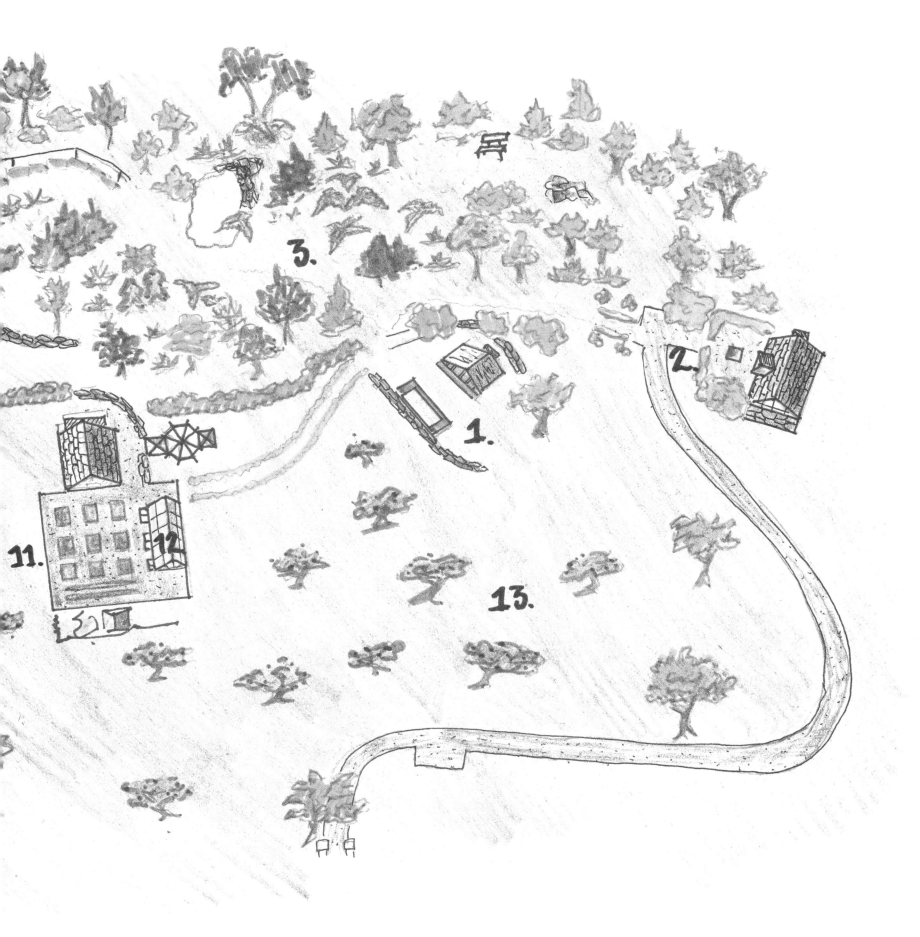

HOUSE GARDEN

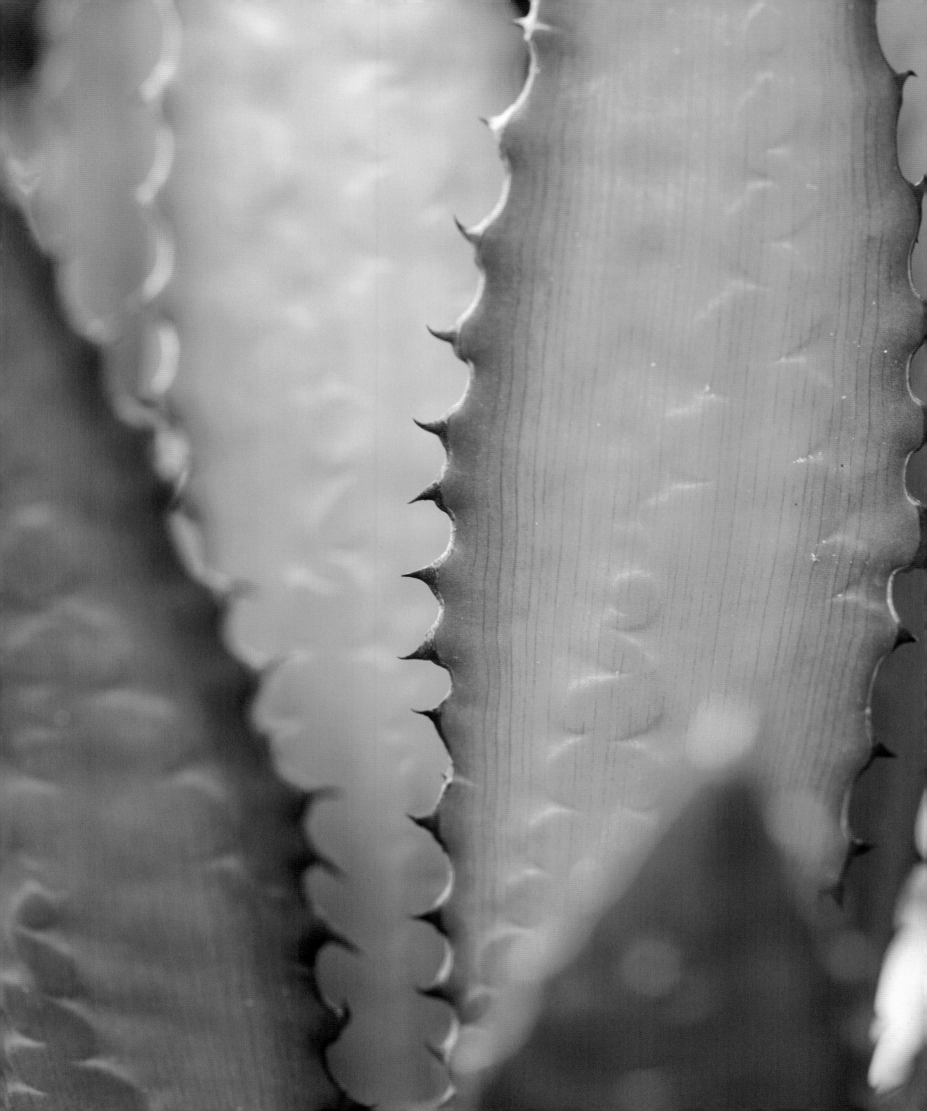

There is no gardening
without humility. Nature
is constantly sending even
its oldest scholars to
the bottom of the class for
some egregious blunder.

—*Alfred Austin*

Looking back on the sunken garden thirty-five years ago when I was starting my gardening journey.

THE SUNKEN GARDEN

From time to time, it is important to stand back and reassess your garden from a different perspective. I had been so busy trying to maintain the big plantings at each end of the sunken garden that I really did not consider the space holistically. As I travelled and was exposed to more and more different gardens, I would come back and take a hard look at my own, often finding it lesser in comparison—lacking in their magic. Everything felt wrong—the gardens were too small for the space, the plants did not read from a distance, the hedgerow that created the south wall was a scrubby mess, and the big lawn that separated the gardens had no . . . soul.

If I wasn't going to revive the lawn tennis court, something more had to be done, so I set about improving the space. I replaced the hedgerow with a row of hemlocks on either side of the lattice arbor that I had built between two old crabapples. This would, eventually, lead to another space, but that came much later.

The borders themselves were deepened to six feet, and I raised the planting beds by adding a modest eighteen-inch stone wall along the front. This gave the plantings more height and scale. Taller plants, like Joe Pye weed, globe thistle, and lemon queen sunflowers to name a few (see complete plant list on page 97) created a grander backdrop. In the middle of the border, we planted phlox, monarda, hibiscus, and aruncus. Along the front of the border, lady's mantle spilled over the low stone wall, mixed with alliums, camas, and echinacea.

But still something was lacking. I decided to add a fishpond in the center, bordered by big flagstones, a low boxwood hedge, and tall arborvitae columns on each corner. John loves to sit on a stone bench and feed the fish— evidently well because they have become huge. But it was on a trip to Normandy, when I was visiting a fabulous garden designed by one of my gardening gurus, Russell Page, that a light went off in my head. Immediately upon my return, I contacted Steve Fitch, an amazing landscaper in Connecticut, and within a few weeks all the grass was removed, and the space was divided into six large planting beds surrounded by boxwood hedging with stone paths in between.

Now, just as in my childhood, the colors emerge in the early spring with large, vibrant alliums, and the bloom lasts until late fall with over forty varieties of perennials. To achieve continuous flowering, we include annuals, such as tall verbena, nicotiana, ageratum, and salvia. For scale and leaf texture, I add canna, castor beans, and cleome.

To augment the nutrients in these densely planted beds, we spread a thick coat of ground-up leaf mulch over the soil after the first frost has come and the plants have been cut back. Over the years, this has made the soil very rich and friable, so

it is easy to plant the annuals in the spring. The leaf mulch also helps to hold moisture in the soil until the time comes to remove some of it so the tiny new shoots can get light.

One thing to think about early on is staking, especially with taller plants. Years ago, when I was visiting Sissinghurst early in the season, I noticed twiggy stems pushed into the bases of the plants; this gives the plants the necessary support at the base, and the stakes are quickly covered over by new foliage. Since then, we save our own apple tree branches after pruning and begin staking when the plants are about twelve inches tall.

The plants grow up through the low branches and have a more natural shape later in the season than they would if you had to support or tie them up. This also saves a lot of time.

After many alterations, this garden is now one of our favorite places to visit late in the afternoon to enjoy a glass of wine, wander, watch the butterflies, and sit on one of the benches and remind ourselves how lucky we are. As much time as we work in our gardens, as much time as we spend seeing what is wrong with them, we need to find at least as much time, if not more, to enjoy them.

PLANTS FOR THE SUNKEN GARDEN

TALL
spotted Joe Pye weed
globe thistle
plume poppy
white fleece flower
Lemon Queen sunflower
sweet coneflower

EVERGREEN COLUMNS
Arborvitae

MID-RANGE
Culver's root
David garden phlox
Helenium Mardi Gras
goatsbeard
white trumpet lily
German bearded iris
purple giant hyssop
coneflower
tree peonies
wild hyacinth

FRONT
lady's mantle
coneflower
phlox
allium tuberosum

HEDGES
Green Velvet boxwood
Green Mountain boxwood

Penhill Dark Monarch
dinnerplate dahlia
Dahlia x *pinnata*
'Penhill Dark Monarch'
Dinnerplate Dahlia

Evening Fragrance
devil's trumpet
Datura innoxia Mill.
'Evening Fragrance'

bugbane
Actaea racemosa L.
(syn. *Cimicifuga racemosa* [L.] Nutt.)

Shirley poppy
Papaver rhoeas Shirley Group

Caribbean Fantasy dahlia
Dahlia 'Caribbean Fantasy'

Sombrero® Sandy Yellow
Coneflower
Echinacea 'Balsomselo'

white trumpet lily
Lilium regale E.H. Wilson

German bearded iris
Iris germanica L.

Big Blue sea holly
Eryngeum x *zabelli* 'Big Blue'

spotted Joe Pye weed
Eutrochium maculatum L.

Ambassador
ornamental onion
Allium 'Ambassador,
Joe-Pye

German bearded iris
Iris germanica L.

THE PARTERRE GARDEN

Over the years, the area that has now become the parterre garden has gone through many transitions. At first, since it was behind the original service barn, it was used as a compost area, which paid off when I decided to locate a vegetable garden in this space. The compost was tilled into the soil, which created a rich growing base for the plants. A barrier was needed to keep out the rabbits, so I chose to build a simple board fence that would weather over time. At the west end of the garden, I had a rustic pergola built to support squash and other vines. Now that the interior garden has become more formal, I sometimes wonder if I should rethink the fence, but with the espalier pear, the climbing roses, and various clematis cascading over it, I cannot bring myself to disrupt them. The pergola is now covered in William Baffin roses.

The parterre was divided into four large beds surrounded by paths made from salvaged bricks that I had amassed years earlier. To my dismay, after a few very cold winters some of the old bricks began to disintegrate. I learned that the lighter-orange bricks did not tolerate frost and needed to be replaced with the much darker red bricks, which have a higher lead content that lets them survive the low temperatures. After twenty-five years, they've acquired the loveliest soft patina of age.

The beds were bordered in tiny ('Green Gem') boxwood, and inside I grew vegetables and herbs that we enjoyed for years. But as things on this property are never static, change was in the air. When John and I decided to renovate the barn and add the conservatory, we wanted to formalize this garden and expand the vegetable garden in another location. The tiny boxwood hedge had grown so much that, even with regular clippings, it was too tall to be practical for vegetables. To transform the space into our parterre garden I started by enclosing it with a hornbeam hedge along the north side to create a back wall that would stop the eye. The parterre garden flourishes from spring through fall but, owing to the structure of the space and the strong pattern of the boxwood hedge, it is just as beautiful in winter when the snow covers it creating a panorama that is especially enjoyable viewed from the warmth of the conservatory. Time has mellowed the fence and the brick paths to the point of looking like they've always been there. In fall we plant tulips for a spring display. We choose from very tall, late-blooming varieties that will reach over the hedge and, ideally, bloom in late May, in time for our first garden tours. After the tulips have finished blooming, they are removed to make space to plant a combination of annuals for summer blooms. Each year we try different colors—most recently pink and orange, but probably my favorite was a mix of white and cream. Another combination that was successful were giant green zinnias and purple salvia. Seamless as it may seem, this requires a great deal of advance planning in the winter months, to order from local growers and ensure enough plants to fill the space.

THE WOODLAND GARDEN

If a thing is worth doing, it is worth doing well. If it is worth having, it is worth waiting for. If it is worth attaining, it is worth fighting for. If it is worth experiencing, it is worth putting aside time for. —Oscar Wilde

After a few years, the sunken garden and the parterre had matured, and as I walked down the path from one to the other, I was inspired to create something new. It dawned on me that at the end of the hornbeam hedge was a fence that, with a gate installed, could lead me to the wooded hillside beyond. It was a very steep hill, so I would set out with some clippers in my pocket and try to cut back a path through the overgrown understory that I hoped would one day make it easy to navigate.

There were wonderful giant rocks covered in moss that dotted the hillside, and at the top of the hill I discovered a giant 150-year-old maple tree that hovered over what seemed like a natural bowl. At the far end were two tall, elegant trees growing out of rock formations. How long they had been there, I could not say, but what I imagined in that spot was a waterfall emerging from the rocks and flowing into a small woodland pond that we would create. Fortunately, a very nice bulldozer operator came to the rescue, moving large stones to create the waterfall I had envisioned. We then stretched a heavy black vinyl liner along the floor of the bowl, added a pump for circulation, and filled the new pond with water. The banks of the pond were planted with primroses, rodgersia, crocuses, and maidenhead ferns. Today, the path that I cleared up the hill brings you to the pond and then around to the pool house and studio beyond. Magical as this transformation may seem, I made many mistakes along the way—a combination of ignorance and haste.

When undertaking a project like this, the first thing to do is eradicate the invasive plants like poison ivy, burning bush, and garlic mustard. The next element to focus on is light. A woodland garden needs pockets of light for ground-level plants to grow, and I soon found that I had to thin out some of the tall trees to create beautiful, dappled light for the low plants. This is not easy to do once those plants are in the ground, so that was one lesson learned. As my woodland had many tall trees, I also had to make room for the understory—comprised of redbuds, dogwoods, hemlocks, American beech, and the like—all needed to give the layered interest the woods lacked.

Another important step is to test your soil. Ours, it turns out, is on a bedrock of lime rocks and is calcareous—chalky, hard, and high in minerals. Over the years, the rich topsoil had been washed away, affecting what I could plant. I did not understand why the thirty or more mountain laurels in the woodland looked so terrible year after year. They thrive on nearby Mount Algo, but they would not grow on this bedrock of limy soil. Azaleas and rhododendron do well there (*rhododendron schlippenbachii* is one of my favorites), and I like the paler-color blooms for the shrubs, rosebay, and oakleaf hydrangea, as they blend beautifully with the woodland's softer natural palette.

When I started, I think I was focused more on creating a shade garden because I had not really seen, or studied, many real woodland gardens. As I wandered along the paths of the Mount Cuba Center in Wilmington, Delaware, I saw native plants used in such a beautiful way and realized this was what I wanted to attempt. No more hostas (I love them, just not in this part of the garden). I wanted to concentrate on native plants that would grow in the new area that I was developing behind the pool house and studio. The first part of the woodland garden is more of a hybrid, with spring bulbs, hellebores, epimedium, and rodgersia (for large leaf texture). Dame's rocket, a beautiful but invasive

plant, mixes itself in with the ferns in late May and must be kept under control with regular weeding.

The woodland starts to come alive in the early spring with hellebores, daffodils, and primroses that continue to bloom until mid-June, but it is still a joy in the middle of the summer when the sun is strong, as it is a cool, serene place to sit in the afternoons. So that we could enjoy the garden from different vantage points, I began collecting faux bois garden benches (cast of cement over wire, to look like they are made of tree branches).

Even though the woodland garden is well established, I am always searching for unusual plants to add. I find that variegated plants lend brightness to the shaded areas later in the summer when there is little in bloom. Some of my favorites are white dogwood, giant dogwood (also called Wedding Cake Tree), and variegated Solomon's Seal.

The woodland is always full of surprises, some good, some bad. Wandering through in the spring is like a scavenger hunt, looking to see, for instance, if the peonies I planted years ago have spread. Luckily, thanks to the squirrels and chipmunks that spread the seeds in the fall, new colonies appear each year. There is constant regeneration, but there are also disasters. When lightning struck the 150-year-old maple tree that first anchored the garden, I wept. I was desperate to tie it back together, but the crack in the trunk reached all the way to the ground and the tree became a safety concern. I did not have another 150 years, and there was no access to bring in another large tree. The solution was to remove the precarious tree and plant three fast-growing sequoias in its place. One must always be prepared for natural disasters in a garden, shed a tear, and move on.

Often John and I will go up to one of the benches in the woodland and just sit and listen. The sounds of the leaves blowing in the breeze and the birds singing to each other are as beautiful as any symphony I have ever heard.

barrenwort
Epimedium L. Epimedium
versicolor 'Sulphureum'

Catawba rhododendron
Rhododendron catawbiense 'Album'

woodland peony
Paeonia obovata

ostrich fern
Matteuccia struthopteris L.

Japanese wood poppy
Glaucidium palmatum
Siebold & Zucc.

yellow lady's slipper orchid
Cypripedium parviflorum Salisb.
var. *pubescens*

Woodland Garden Maintenance

FALL

Once the trees have shed their leaves, Robert mows the woodland with a brush mower. Large branches are chipped and spread back with the mulch to encourage a rich forest floor.

WINTER

Pruning or thinning trees is healthy for them and allows more sunlight to come in for the understory.

SPRING

Seasonal weeding begins, of particular concern in our area are garlic mustard (that should not be allowed to seed), poison ivy, wild parsley, and narrow leaf butter cress (cardamine impatiens).

Lastly, remember to leave fallen logs to encourage fungi (mushrooms) that are most beneficial to the ecosystem of the woodlands.

THE ORCHARD

Years after buying the house, I was able to acquire the adjacent field that had originally been part of the property. Later, when John and I decided to build the swimming pool and temple pavilion, I wanted to add a few apple trees on the hill that slopes down from there. Knowing he was an expert on apples, I reached out to Dennis Mareb of Windy Hill Nursery—from whom I had bought many other wonderful trees and shrubs—about purchasing a couple of trees. A few weeks later, he called to say that he had been offered an entire mature orchard (about to be destroyed for development), and he could dig up the trees and plant them immediately at a more reasonable cost than planting young trees. I did not need a full orchard, but could not resist the large trees, with their gracious branches and heritage apples of multiple varieties. Under Dennis' guidance, they were delivered and planted in rows and voilà: an orchard on the hillside. The majesty of these trees, skillfully pruned over many years, in full bloom in the spring, makes my heart stop. I want those blossoms to last forever, but they are ephemeral and that makes them even more special. For me, apple trees are living sculptures; no two are alike, and the older they get the more beautiful they become. We have since added cherries and peaches to the orchard so, hopefully, late in the summer we will have plenty of fruit to make tarts, crisps, jams, and chutneys.

Under the orchard trees, I asked Robert if I could have a field of mostly Queen Anne's lace, one of my most favorite flowers—a large bouquet of it is a dream. He started prepping the site by dragging a scarifying rake over the ground to remove the existing thatch and expose bare soil. The seed was then sown in December 2018 and, because Queen Anne's lace is biennial, it flowered in the summer of 2020. I truly love wandering along the grass paths through the orchard and marveling at the thousands of delicate flowers that look like giant snowflakes blowing in the breeze.

In the past, the field was mowed once in the winter, but now Robert is considering a late-spring mowing to prevent invasives like mugwort and multiflora rose from coming in, as well as to stop the late-summer succession of old-field goldenrod that interrupts the natural life cycle of insects. In the meantime, patches of milkweed have appeared to the delight of the monarch butterflies.

The backdrop of the orchard is the rusticated pool house that I built more than twenty-five years ago. Inspired by Greek revival architecture and a photograph of a log porch that I had saved, I envisioned a Greek temple made from the adjacent woods, and it is from there that we now overlook the orchard.

'Green fingers' are a fact, and a
mystery only to the unpracticed.
But green fingers are the extensions
of a verdant heart. A good garden
cannot be made by somebody
who has not developed the capacity
to know and love growing things.

— *Russell Page*

Robert giving me instructions for repotting in the greenhouse.

THE WORKING GARDEN

John and I had repurposed the original barn to become a space for entertaining, so I was faced with the dilemma of what to do with all the equipment that we had acquired to maintain our expanding garden. When I visited other properties, I was always drawn to the back where all the mowers, wheelbarrows, carts, and tools were stored amid stacks of terra-cotta pots and rich bins of compost. This is where it all begins.

I located a spot on the property where I could create a complex with a barn, a greenhouse, and a large vegetable and cutting garden. I have always loved barns, and it was important that our new barn would look as though it had always been there. Down the road from our house was a 19th-century barn that I had always loved, so I used it as inspiration. For consistency, I felt that all the outbuildings should be the same color. When I renovated the original 18th-century barn, I chose a dull green for the siding and a slightly lighter color for the trim. It was a Cabot stain that they do not make anymore, but the closest colors are Benjamin Moore Hancock Gray HC-97 for the siding and Camouflage 2143-40 for the trim. When I built the new barn, the greenhouse, the chicken coop, and later my studio, I had them all painted in the same colors so they would not only match, but also blend into the landscape.

Because there is a hill to the west of where the barn would be built, we had to dig out the bank and build a retaining wall. The new barn has two large bays: One side has space for the mowers and heavy equipment, along with winter storage in the back for the large oil jars and clay pots that cannot stay out in the cold, plus a wall where the rakes, shovels, and spades are hung. In the second bay, we built shelves for storage of the many pots I have collected over the years, while a long worktable adjacent to the back wall holds all the smaller tools. There are also bundles of bamboo stakes needed to support plants, balls of twine, bags of potting soil, and shelves for all the fertilizer. As the saying goes, "a place for everything, and everything in its place."

On the east side of the barn was a flat space that was perfect for the vegetable garden and a long greenhouse. The site gets full sun, which is ideal for growing. On the far side, however, I was limited by three ancient apple trees that I could not bring myself to cut down, so I staked out the plot for the vegetable and cutting gardens and chose a spot for the greenhouse on the north side. I ordered a commercial vinyl greenhouse measuring fifty by twenty-five feet, which was the largest I could manage at the time, but it has been amazing. The automatic vents and heaters work perfectly, and I later added a generator in case of power outages, which are frequent during snowstorms. On the south side of the greenhouse are large rolling tables that allow maximum surface area for the plants, and I built stacked shelving along the north side for additional space. In the fall we can store dormant bulbs for forcing in the late winter. The exterior of the greenhouse was not very attractive, so I added an open pattern of wooden lathing strips to add interest while hiding the vinyl panels. Along the south side of the greenhouse, I installed four large cold frames, which were dug into the ground and covered with repurposed old windows. The garden had to be fenced to keep out the wild rabbits (who are especially fond of young, tender plants), and I was so lucky when my friend Bob Willington, an antiques dealer in Maine, offered me a wonderful old fence he had salvaged that was perfect for the space. I love repurposing elements that give the illusion that they have been there for years.

The vegetable garden measures about eighty-three by sixty-six feet and is laid out in nine square beds, plus two rectangular ones along the east end. I've always loved the French potagers, especially the ones in Villandry, so each spring, Tricia Van Oers (who is now our main gardener) and I plan the layout of each bed. Tricia's favorite vegetables (a list of which is on page 187) are mixed in with the flowers I most like cutting to bring into the house. The tulips and fritillaria, planted in the fall, are the first to arrive. Once they bloom, the bulbs are removed to make way for the vegetables and other cutting flowers. There is a long bed of peonies, which come back year after year. In the early spring we plant the dahlias and other tall annuals. Later in the summer, foxgloves, delphinium, zinnias, lilies, and sunflowers (see complete list on page 187) provide buckets full of flowers for arranging throughout the season. The center bed of the vegetable garden is reserved for the herbs we use for cooking, including rosemary, dill, and chives.

The last addition to the working garden was a small potting shed that I rescued from the end of the long wing of the main house when I had to make a space for a new first-floor bedroom. I could not bear to destroy this lovely 18th-century shed, so we had it moved with a crane to this new location. This gave me a perfect place to work and to store my favorite pots, tools, and extensive collection of baskets and old watering cans. It's become one of my favorite spots—there are a table and chairs for sitting down to lunch, and benches for enjoying an early morning coffee or a break from gardening, harvesting vegetables, and cutting flowers.

globe amaranth
Gomphrena QIS™
Formula Mix

Adirondack Red potato
Solanum tuberosum
'Adirondack Red'

Aswad eggplant
Solanum melongena 'Aswad'

rosemary
Salvia rosmarinus
(previously known as
Rosmarinus officinalis)

Hachi lily
Lilium 'Hachi'

San Marzano tomato
Solanum lycopersicum
'San Marzano'

VEGETABLE AND CUTTING GARDEN MAINTENANCE

Tricia Van Oers, who so beautifully maintains the vegetable and cutting garden, outlined the following schedule for garden care:

EARLY SPRING

First, remove some mulch where seeds are to be planted. Kale, cabbage, lettuces, parsley, and chard are great to begin with.

Build trellis supports with long bamboo poles and twine for tomatoes and shelling peas.

When setting out plants, use a granular fertilizer and side dress with compost. If they need a boost during the season, use an organic liquid fish fertilizer. Bone meal is best for onions.

Cabbages should be sprayed weekly with B.t. dissolved in water to prevent cabbage caterpillars. Hand pick cucumber beetles and squash bugs.

Hygiene in the garden is very important. Spray natural fungicide to slow down leaf disease. Make sure to remove any diseased leaves.

Soil should be covered with a thick layer of mulch to keep down weeds and hold in moisture.

FALL

After a hard frost, remove any dead plants.

Plan your layout for next year's planting.

Prepare beds for tulips, garlic, and any other bulbs and plant them.

Cover the soil with two inches of a protective layer of leaf mulch, to keep the ground from freezing (over the years it is leaf mulch that has made our soil so rich).

Our favorite sources for seeds are Johnny's Selected Seeds, Baker Creek Heirloom Seed Company, and High Mowing Organic Seeds.

Tricia's Favorite Vegetable Varieties

Maxibel haricot vert
French filet-bean bush

Belstar broccoli
long season, vigorous growth

Caraflex cabbage
easy-to-grow green cabbage

Napoli carrot
Nantes-type carrot with
a long season

Silverado Swiss chard
great from spring till frost

Poona Kheera cucumber
yellow, crunchy, and sweet

Aswad eggplant
large, sweet, and tender

Music garlic
flavorful Italian Porcelain
variety

Redbor kale
red frilly-leafed kale

Alisa Craig onion
large, sweet yellow onion

Carmen pepper
Italian red sweet pepper

Sungold tomato
sweet golden cherry tomato

Rose de Berne tomato
flavorful pink heirloom variety

San Marzano tomato
classic Italian plum tomato

Moss Curled parsley
classic ruffled parsley,
also nice in bouquets

My Favorite Annuals for Cutting

Hopi Red Dye amaranth
Green Mist ammi
Inky Fingers coleus
Smallwood's Orange coleus
cosmos
Blue Spires delphinium

foxglove
Lemon Lime ageratum
Espresso gladiolus
All Around Purple globe
amaranth Gomphrena

spotted beebalm
silver spurflower
black pincushion flower
Queen Lime Orange zinnia
Queen Lime Red zinnia

THE GARDEN IN WINTER

Like life itself, I wish I could slow down the garden season. In early spring, we bundle up to see if the young hellebores are poking up through the cold, damp mulch. Beginning in early chill of fall when leaves start to change, John and I wander until the frost comes and, with it, my time to explore the bones of the garden, to review the last season, and to start making plans for the spring.

During winter walks, I find time for true reflection. The clipped hedges, the arbors, the gravel and mulched paths, the fences that surround the various gardens all give winter interest. The twisted shapes of the meticulously pruned apple trees, the texture on the bark of the old locust, maples, and hinkle trees, and the majestic columns of the arborvitae can be better appreciated when their surroundings are dormant. It is then that we can see potential, as—thank heavens—a garden is never done.

The winter is also a good time to do site work, like creating paths, terraces, or digging a new bed. I am not one to keep a detailed garden journal, but I do take many photographs, especially where I see room for improvement. This year, for instance, the sunken garden was a melody of purples, so Robert and I decided to add pale yellow iris and baptisia.

We are very fortunate to have indoor spaces to retreat to during the winter months. The conservatory has begun to feel (in my imagination) like the hanging gardens of Babylon, with vines weaving through clear fishing line supports that cascade over the windows. Pedestals of various heights hold a variety of begonia rex orchids, while an asparagus fern climbs through a huge palm to reach the skylights on the ceiling. This is a perfect spot for lunch on a sunny winter day, and I can often be found in one of the comfortable wicker chairs with stacks of garden books, catalogs, and my iPad.

While we can entertain in the conservatory, the greenhouse is where I can do some real winter gardening. The building is jam-packed with all the tender plants that need to be kept from the cold. Though Robert manages with great effort to keep each plant looking perfect, and the bugs to a minimum, I can always find something to do. Nothing is more relaxing than spending a few hours, listening to glorious music while dead heading, repotting, rooting new cuttings, trimming the standards, and inhaling the delicious scents of jasmine and citrus.

Sow the seeds of Victory!
plant &
raise
your own
vegetables

"Every Garden a Munition Plant"

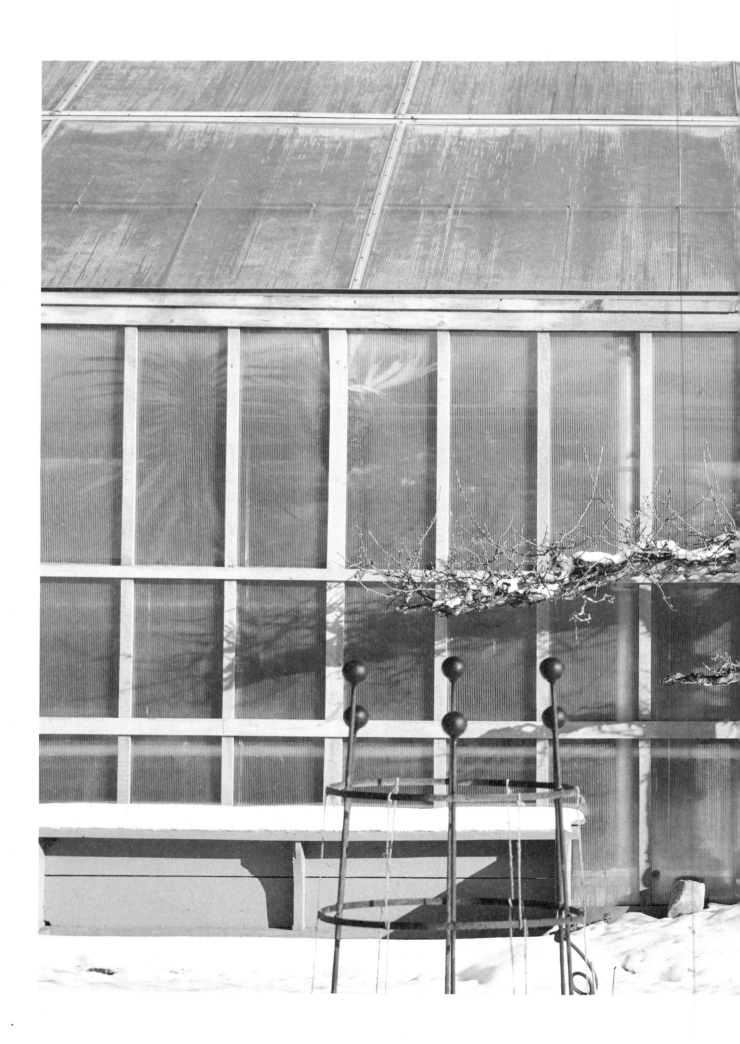

dancing-lady orchid
Oncidium

orange snowball cactus
Rebutia muscula
F.Ritter & P.Thiele

Red Star cordyline
Cordyline australis 'Red Star'

pink orchid cactus
Disocactus phyllanthoides

Meyer lemon
Citrus x *meyeri*

Jollies Nantes fuchsia
Fuchsia x *hybrida*
'Jollies Nantes'

mountain cowslip
Primula auricula

red mistletoe cactus
Pseudorhipsalis ramulosa

Mrs. Cox geranium
Pelargonium x *hortorum*
'Mrs. Cox'

Elegance™ Imperial
geranium
Pelargonium x *domesticum*
'Elegance™ Imperial'

donkey's tail
Sedum morganium

queen of the night cactus
Epiphyllum oxypetalum

Until we can comprehend
the beguiling beauty of a
single flower, we are woefully
unable to grasp the meaning
and potential of life itself.

—*Virginia Woolf*

FLOWER ARRANGING

From the very first time I set foot in a museum, I was drawn to paintings of flowers, from the still lifes of 16th- and 17th-century Dutch and Italian masters to later works by Henri Fantin-Latour, Édouard Manet, and Mary Cassatt. I would spend time studying not only the painting technique, but also the arrangement of flowers. Art has always been an inspiration for me and, even now, when I see a picture of an interesting bouquet, I like to cut it out and pin it to the inspiration board in my studio. There is no better way to enliven a room than by bringing in flowers and plants.

I am not a master florist; in fact, I like my arrangements to be loose and to feel as though I just went outside with my clippers, gathered a bunch of flowers in my hand, and dropped them into a vase. Each summer weekend, early in the morning when it is cooler, the flowers, flowering shrubs, and greenery are cut and put into tin or black plastic buckets to soak up all the water they need, and later in the day I go to work. Arranging flowers is truly one of my favorite things to do. I find it ever so calming to focus on combining colors and textures. It's like painting a picture without the pressure, flowers are already perfect. I deliberately compose arrangements for the center of the kitchen, and dining table, and smaller ones for accents around the house. We usually have two taller compositions for the entrance and the barn, where the ceiling is highest. I love the way they draw the eye up and create an exciting sense of scale.

Throughout the years of developing the garden plan, I have always found a place for the small trees and shrubs that I know I'll want on hand for flower arranging. Lilacs, hydrangeas, spirea, and viburnum are some of my favorites. I also planted a big stand of false spirea, which is the best filler for any size arrangement as it has the most beautiful arching branches. Even though we have an endless variety of flowers in our garden, I am never without my clippers when driving around the neighborhood. You would be surprised how many wonderful things there are to cut along the side of the road when you start looking. Either way, between the early hellebores, daffodils, and spring-flowering shrubs and trees, the tulips planted in the fall, and the annuals intended for cutting, there is a constant supply of flowers until the late fall, when we begin to fill the house with plants grown in the greenhouse.

Over time I have amassed a huge collection of containers. Some of my favorites are antique lusterware pitchers and Chinese export mugs. There are new pieces from one of my favorite ceramicists, Lila Francis Pottery, and from Astier de Villatte. I have a full range of different vessels in every imaginable color, shape, and size, from vases with a tall, narrow neck where I can put a particular flower like a tree peony blossom or a single iris, to smaller ones—like a collection of tiny blue and white jars that I can arrange with the same flower down the center of the dining table with candlelight in between, or the

small colored glass vases that I set across one of the mantlepieces. Having containers of various sizes is very important and makes arranging flowers so much easier. If decorating a dining table, you want to have containers that are no more than eight inches high so people can see each other over the flowers.

In some places I consistently use the same vase, such as a large blue and white Chinese jar that's perfect for the grand arrangement on the front hall table. On the desk in the barn, I used a huge brown Aptware urn for years until it produced a big crack from the weight of the water and flowers. It was repaired and moved to the top of a nearby cabinet, and its role on the desk is now filled by a large fiberglass urn that looks like stone and is better suited to the weight.

Even though I love to experiment with more imposing volumes, at times I get the greatest pleasure from the simplicity of a beautiful branch in a tall glass vase like the ones I buy from Jamali Floral & Garden Supplies in Chelsea. Each weekend we cut a long branch from the woods to go in the center of the large table in my studio. When I'm pressed for time, the scale of a tall branch can also make a dramatic statement in the front hall in lieu of a full arrangement.

When I begin to work with a group of flowers, I first consider the shape of vase. Those that have a narrow opening and wider base (pitchers, teapots, or fishbowl shapes) offer plenty of support for stems. For those that do not (flared vases, urns, glass cubes, or any more open shapes) I have amassed a collection of "frogs." While I enjoy these as objects, in the end, what I find most effective is chicken wire: I bunch

it up to fit inside the container and attach it to the sides with floral tape so I can slip the stems through the web of wires. This method allows me greater freedom to create the most natural arrangements with stems of any size. To make a bouquet last longer, I remove all the leaves from the stems that will be submerged, check the water every day and change it, cut the stems, and add plant food, as needed.

Since I so enjoy arranging flowers, I created a small area off the kitchen just for that purpose. Above a marble-top counter with a sink, I mounted long shelves that hold many of my containers while, in drawers underneath, I keep my clippers, scissors, frogs, and chicken wire so everything I need is within reach. In our apartment in the city—where I often buy flowers at the corner deli—I do my arrangements in the kitchen too. If you don't grow your own—or want more variety—cut flowers can also be found at local farmer's markets throughout summer.

If you are not comfortable doing flowers, I suggest assembling a collection of bud vases and bottle neck vases of various sizes. You can cut blossoms to size for each vase and group them together. I have some tall vases that I can place on a side table with just one beautiful lily or a huge dahlia blossom, and there is nothing prettier. Flower arranging should be a joy, but if it feels intimidating, or like too much work, bringing live plants into the house is a very effective alternative. I have a large collection of cachepots that I can simply drop a potted plant into. An orchid, a standard bay tree, a glorious blooming geranium, or even a lovely fern is all it takes to make a room come alive.

CONTAINER PLANTING

If one day I had to give up this garden, I know I could be happy with a small terrace filled with containers where I could grow some of my favorite flowers and plants. When thoughtfully arranged and planted with harmonious colors, they can create a garden in the smallest of spaces.

As in many country homes, we find ourselves using the side door as our main entrance because it is close to where we park our cars, in a courtyard shaded by a huge maple tree. Nothing would grow in the soil there, so I laid a flagstone terrace inside the picket fence with the large tree in the center. Every year, we bring plants out from the greenhouse; boxwood balls in terra-cotta pots and a large sago palm, which is placed in one corner. Along the wall of the house, under the kitchen window, a long metal table is filled with pots of begonias, petunias, and ivy that spills over the edge. A pair of tall myrtle standards marks the entrance, and beneath them are pots of annuals, such as salvia and foxgloves. I often change out these pots with plants I find in the nursery, but always limit my palette to greens, yellows, and purples. In the winter, they are replaced with small evergreens.

Throughout the property, I place containers along walkways and on stone walls to draw the eye. Leading from the side door around the house, the containers and plants add interest to the paths. Along the north side of the new addition, two pedestals with large, black iron urns filled with giant ferns frame a metal garden bench. In the summertime, the side path becomes home to two big orange trees and Versailles boxes filled with agapanthus. I also use containers to punctuate an area going into the sunken garden, with four square planters with boxwood balls acting almost like finials. On top of the new walls are three stone planters with annuals, and along the perimeter of the sunken garden, we space twelve boxwood balls in terra-cotta pots on either side of the teak garden benches. The containers add dimension, and as the garden is filled with color and texture, the clipped boxwood balls lend contrast. We are lucky

to have the greenhouse, where many of these plants live during the winter as hardiness is a crucial consideration.

I like to grow most of our small plants in terra-cotta pots, particularly the paler rosy ones from Italy. I also love the handcrafted pots made by local potter Guy Wolff and his son, Benjamin, who create lovely soft-gray pots of all sizes. The choice of vessel is very important. If you want to leave them out year-round (and you live in a freezing zone), choose stone, wood, lead, iron, or fiberglass. I have purchased several fabulous fiberglass containers from Pennoyer Newman, far easier to move since they are not as heavy as the lead ones. I've had the same two iron urns on my front terrace for years; in the warm months I fill them with large ferns or acanthus, and as winter approaches I replant them with small evergreen trees that I can wrap with small white lights at Christmastime.

If I am doing a grouping, I like all the pots to be the same color and to complement their surroundings. As my house is traditional white clapboard, I like natural materials. If I use wooden boxes or planters, I paint them either very dark green, almost black, or white to blend in. I am not a fan of highly decorated pots because I prefer to showcase the plants. In a stone trough, I create little gardens of mixed succulents. For height, I tie tall bamboo stakes together in a wooden Versailles planter and train morning glories, passionflower, or even small cherry tomato vines through the twine that wraps around the stakes for stability. When we open the screened porch in summer, I fill the tables with begonias and ferns that do well in the shade and use tall pedestals with ivy standards and larger ferns to draw the eye upward.

One of the great things about container gardening is creating your own collection of vessels. I can never resist a hand-thrown clay pot, a simple metal urn, or a lovely old wooden planter box. My collection has grown over the years, and I so enjoy deciding which ones to use each spring. It's wonderful to watch the plants and flowers flourish over the coming months, as before I know it, it's time to get out the catalogs, sit by the fireplace, and start planning for next spring and summer.

floating fern
Azolla filiculoides subsp. *cristata*

mammoth pansy
Viola 'Mammoth Mix'

galaxy petunia
Petunia 'Night Sky'

'Vancouver™ Mystic
Gem' clematis
Clematis 'Vancouver™
Mystic Gem'

geranium
Pelargonium 'Platinum'

lily of the Nile
Agapanthus africanus

kiss-me-over-the-
garden-gate
Persicaria orientalis L. Spach

foxtail lily
Eremerus ruiter x *E. isabellinus*
'Ruiter's Hybrid Mix'

black-eyed Susan
Rudbeckia hirta 'Becky' mix

Café au Lait dahlia
Dahlia 'Café au Lait'
Dinnerplate Dahlia

peony
Paeonia var.

Guardian Blue larkspur
Delphinum elatum
'Guardian Blue'

In garden arrangement, as in all other kinds of decorative work, one has not only to acquire a knowledge of what to do, but also gain some wisdom in perceiving what is it well to let alone.

— *Gertrude Jekyll*

ENTERTAINING

If you were lucky enough to grow up in the South, hospitality is something that you learned about early on. From christening, birthday, and engagement parties to Easter egg rolls and large cocktail buffets where all age groups were included, there just seemed to be something exciting and sociable happening all the time. After church on Sundays, we would go to my favorite Aunt Berta's for lunch, where there could be as many as twenty places set at the grown-ups' table. I remember thinking that I would never get to move from the children's table to the dining room. I have always loved parties and was fortunate to participate in the planning with my mother and her friends; for me, it is still the most fun.

When I got my first apartment in New York, with my dear friend Pammy Hobson, we could not wait to have a party. We had a tiny apartment and very limited resources, but we would invite our friends, who would bring more friends, and we would serve "Tuna Wiggle Casserole" (noodles, a can of tuna, a can of mushroom soup, and a can of green peas with saltine crackers on top) and plenty of inexpensive wine to as many people as would fit. Everyone had a fabulous time. It's not always about the food; it is the effort of bringing people together that makes a party.

I was truly blessed when I married John Rosselli, as one of the many wonderful things about John is that he is an extraordinary cook. John is the youngest of fourteen in an Italian family, and his oldest sister had a restaurant where he worked after school. John is a truly natural cook. He reads cookbooks and watches cooking shows, but when he is in the kitchen, he is like a great orchestra conductor. A little more of this, a little less of that. He can prepare a meal for eighteen in a few hours, with a perfectly immaculate kitchen when the food comes to the table. I tried to do a cookbook with him, but it was impossible because he never measures anything. John was horrified when I told him about my first dinner parties with tuna casserole.

As cooking is John's sport, he always wants to have a reason to be in the kitchen, so our house is often filled with guests, sometimes for the entire weekend, or at least for a lunch or dinner. And as he does not want me in the kitchen, he says, "Go do your tablescapes."

Entertaining is very easy when you are prepared. I must confess that, after many years of collecting, I have three pantries filled with china, glasses, napkins, tablecloths, and silverware. What is amazing to me is that if you are enthusiastic shoppers like we are, you can find such interesting things in secondhand shops and at auctions. My stacks of vintage white damask dinner napkins have been collected over time from various sources. One thing I try to do to control my buying is to keep to a color scheme or two, as I like to mix things together. John loves blue and white china, so we have plates, bowls, and platters in various patterns, from early Canton ware and Wedgewood to contemporary pieces from Christopher Spitzmiller, as well as inexpensive Japanese bowls from Pearl River Mart in New York City. When they're all layered together, it not only looks fabulous, but we have enough place settings for eight or forty-eight. I do the same with floral pieces, always trying to combine colors and patterns that work together. We also have a mixture of colorful pottery pieces for informal lunches and a large collection of tablecloths, everything from repurposed Indian bedspreads to simple white linen. I have them in many colors, patterns, and sizes to fit over the different tables throughout the house and gardens. I feel like this is my paint box, as I am mixing patterns and colors. It is as close as I can get to painting like Henri Matisse.

For flatware, I use family silver, coin silver that John and I have collected over the years, and the modern bamboo flatware I created for Ballard Designs. Our glasses, too, come from many different sources— from crystal for formal dinners to hand-blown glasses bought in Egypt and Morocco.

We entertain informally. John cooks, and the food is served on a large buffet. Guests help themselves and then go to the table, where I always have place cards. I plan the seating ahead of time because I think guests feel more comfortable when they know where to sit. If there is

a large group, we'll hire professionals to pass around seconds, clear the table, serve dessert, and lend a hand with cleanup. This way, we can spend more time with our guests. What I love most is sitting around the table after dinner, chatting away.

The most important entertaining advice I can give is to plan. Do everything in advance so that you are relaxed and can be a participant in your own party—a harried host makes everyone uncomfortable. Sometimes we invite people a few weeks in advance, but we often host last-minute gatherings too because we've had so much practice. I plan the seating, set the tables, and do the flowers a full day before, and John and I (mostly John) decide on a menu. John prepares the meals ahead of time, so they only need reheating, and when the guests arrive, he's always dressed (beautifully, I might add) and ready to have a great time.

We have a large drinks table where everyone helps themselves (except when there are a lot of guests, and we hire a bartender). Everything is there, all kinds of liquors, mixes, wine, Perrier, and glasses set out on a tray. If we are having a dinner, I don't serve a lot of hors d'oeuvres, just bowls of good Virginia peanuts, cheese straws in baskets, and maybe a large board with cheese, crackers, and thinly sliced good Italian salami or a big plate of crudités. As guests wander around, they can help themselves. For a cocktail buffet, we have small plates and only serve food that can be eaten with a fork. It is impossible to cut food with a plate on your lap.

Another important thing to consider is lighting. I have been in too many lovely rooms ruined by too much light. In our dining room, or the conservatory, or even the kitchen, I always lower any overhead fixtures and light the table with either votive candles or the LED Pina Pro Lamp from Lumens. It's magic, the way it lights the tabletop and flowers clearly while casting only a warm glow on people's faces. This adds some ambiance to a dinner, and who doesn't like a bit of romance?

Over the years, John and I have really enjoyed hosting large events in support of local charities. Since they are fundraisers, we want to make sure the evening is special, and that does take advance planning. Typically, we will call on our favorite caterer, Rita Welch, to provide food and

drinks, and do the rest by ourselves. I call my dear stylist friend Howard Christian, my first creative director, to help decorate the round tent that we can set up between the curved hedges on the lawn behind the house. Often, volunteers from the charity will also lend a hand. It takes a lot of them to cut buckets full of flowers from the garden, bloom branches from the trees, and scour nearby roadsides for wildflowers. My favorite electrician, John Gillette, lights the tent, either with huge color Japanese paper lanterns, or spotlights on huge pedestals that hold giant fiberglass urns filled with blossoming branches and tall flowers. I cover the tables with my Indian painted bedspreads and fill containers from my collection with mixed bouquets of garden-grown flowers alongside small potted plants from the greenhouse.

Of course, the most special event we ever hosted was the wedding of my nephew, Carter Blackwell, and his fiancée, Kate Cardoza. The pool house served as a chapel for the ceremony, after which the guests walked down through the woodlands to the parterre garden for cocktails and music. Then we moved around the house for dinner in the round tent. After dinner, toasts, and wedding cake, a fabulous DJ had us dancing until the wee hours of the morning. Bringing people together is such fun, but the real joy for me is in the creation of the event.

Elegance™ Imperial geranium
Pelargonium x *domesticum*
'Elegance™ Imperial'

Love-Lies-Bleeding
Amaranthus caudatus
var. *gibbosus*

Benary's Giant Purple
zinnia
Zinnia elegans
'Benary's Giant Purple'

Camelot Lavender foxglove
Digitalis purpurea
'Camelot Lavender'

Camelot Lavender foxglove
Digitalis purpurea
'Camelot Lavender'

Green Twister coneflower,
zinnia, coleus bouquet
Echinacea purpurea
'Green Twister'

302

black pincushion flower
Scabiosa atropurpurea syn.
Sixalix atropurpurea
'Black Knight'

Alice du Pont rock trumpet
Mandevilla x *amabilis*
'Alice du Pont'

Purple Elegance tulip
Tulipa 'Purple Elegance'

Red Lake red currant
Ribes rubrum 'Red Lake'

Royal Purple smoke tree
Cotinus coggygria
'Royal Purple'

Goldflame honeysuckle
Lonicera x *heckrottii* 'Goldflame'

And don't think the
garden loses its ecstasy
in winter. It's quiet,
but the roots are down
there riotous.   —*Rumi*

CHRISTMAS

My mother loved everything about Christmas, so as a child I got caught up in the excitement months in advance. The planning began early in the fall. My mother set up long tables in our third-floor attic, where she was joined once a week by her friends to create magical items to be sold in the annual church Christmas bazaar: ornaments made of cardboard cut into circles, stars, trees, and triangles and covered with metal papers, gold ribbons, and brightly colored stones; Christmas stockings pieced from old fabrics they had collected over the year; and exquisite wreaths and garlands of magnolia leaves and boxwood from the garden, embellished with pinecones, dried baby's breath, berries, and twigs. I loved to be allowed to help with these projects. The attic was a busy workshop for months.

We often went out to the field with my father to pick a Christmas tree to put in front of the big picture window in the living room. It was so thrilling to open the boxes where the decorations had been carefully stored and then hang them on the branches. I loved it when we would turn off the lamps, sit by the fire, and gaze at the glowing tree covered in tiny lights, glittery balls, tinsel, and the many unique ornaments that mommy had collected over the years. I still love trees that have not been pruned into a pyramidal shape as they allow spaces between the branches to hang the baubles. Sadly, they are getting harder and harder to find.

The Christmas pageant at St. Paul's Ivy Church was a main event of the Christmas season. There was a live nativity scene, and all the children of the parish participated. I was among the youngest, and we were dressed as angels, with white gauze dresses and tinsel halos, standing in front of the choir behind the altar. While the choir and congregation sang beautiful hymns, the older children came down the aisle dressed as wise men, peasants, and princes, followed by the Angel of the Annunciation, Mary, and Joseph. Once the stage was set, the Reverend Dudley Booker would tell the story of the birth of Christ. This is where the seed of my love for the nativity was planted. When I was a teenager, my parents brought me to

New York City for Christmas and took me to the Metropolitan Museum of Art to see their magnificent Christmas tree, which was surrounded by the most exquisite Neapolitan baroque nativity scene I had ever seen. This was the 233-figure collection that Loretta Hines Howard began in 1925 and bequeathed to the museum in 1964, starting a tradition that is still carried on by her family and the Metropolitan Museum today.

The Christmas tradition of nativity scenes, or crèches, to depict the birth of Jesus began in 18th-century Naples, then an artistic center famous for its artisans. Originally commissioned by noble families, the scenes were crafted by the finest sculptors, and the figures wore costumes made of fabrics from the royal silk factory in San Leucio. Artisans who specialized in costuming, jewelry, silversmithing, and wood carving contributed to making the figures, while animals were carved by artists skilled in naturalistic representations. No detail was left undone, from the beautiful bronze collar on a dog to the exquisite facial expression of an angel. Today along the Via San Gregorio Armeno, in the center of Naples's historic district, there are hundreds of shops where artisans still carve, mold, and paint the figures for locals and visitors to purchase.

When John and I opened our shop, Treillage, in New York City, we started going to every antique show we could manage, and in France, England, and Belgium I saw crèche figurines for sale. I was drawn to them by their artistry, their detail, and their beauty and I could not resist them, so I began to collect one piece at a time. As my collection grew, I realized I needed to make a real display of all the pieces. I cleared a large marble-top console in the conservatory and used it to stage my collection. However, it was through the vision of Jonathan Preece, who has been our creative director at Bunny Williams Inc. for twenty-six years, that the magic began to happen. Jonathan is as passionate about crèches as I am, as we both love their theater and artistry. He puts a great deal of effort into building platforms for each grouping of villagers with their fruits and vegetables, and shepherds with their animals, and a gothic pergola where Mary and Joseph look down at the manger while papier-mâché angels that John decorated years ago for the Lenox Hill Christmas bazaar hang overhead. Jonathan

covers the stands with bark and moss, while stones and sand create the landscape. This takes at least four long days to set up, but when the hidden lights go on at night, I sit and look in amazement. It's at times like this that I recall my childhood and Christmases of the past. When we have dinner in this room, guests never want to leave the table.

I like a natural Christmas tree, and we place ours in the barn (as we call it, it's really a party space) because it has tall ceilings that can accommodate a thirteen-foot tree. The ornaments I have collected for years, come from every imaginable place, and consist of carved animals, gilded beads, crochet dolls, plenty of bunnies, and many sparkly glass baubles hung on ribbons. It takes several days to get them all onto the tree (and I can't possibly reach the top), so we hire a group to help me, Robert Reimer, my lead gardener, and Jennifer Majette, my housekeeper and gardener, who are integral to the effort. In fact, it is Robert who finds a huge tree and has it installed for us to decorate—and he's likely to have earmarked next year's tree already. What fun it is to turn on beautiful music and, starting at the top, fill in all the branches.

Throughout the house we decorate all the mantels—being an old house, there is a fireplace in every room. I combine my collection of Christmas objects with pine boughs, hollies, and some of the unusual colored evergreens that I intentionally planted along the back fence to use for holiday decorations. Alongside dried pomegranates, apples, and pinecones, I tuck in some of the birds' nests I save when they fall from trees. Every mantel is different, and the house always looks so bare after we put all the decorations away in January.

Outside there are grand wreaths on the doors and a garland of white pine branches and pinecones draped along the picket fence. Small white lights wrap little trees planted in urns by the doors to the barn for a festive welcome. My family, my nieces and nephew (and now their children), have been a part of our life in this house since we bought it, and I'm always excited when we can be together this time of year. Christmas morning is a beehive of activity when gifts are passed out from under the tree and stockings are emptied. Just as my mother and father created so many memories for me, I hope to be doing the same for the next generation.

Magic-making at Aunt Bunny's

Carter Blackwell

The route from Boston is etched in my mind. As a kid, I remember taking the Massachusetts Turnpike to the Lee/Exit 2 and then beginning an extended series of jogs and turns, crossing numerous railroad tracks, passing the Red Lion Inn in Stockbridge, and rolling through Great Barrington and the Berkshires, right after the hot dog stand in Canaan, followed by a left up a hill, and that was when I knew we were close. I can remember the forks in the road—a left here, a right over the tracks there—and the drive through a large farm nestled in a valley. Beyond the farm it was all open fields until, after passing a cemetery on the left, we'd round a left-hand turn down the hill and arrive at Aunt Bunny's. No matter how many times we drove that route, the moment I laid my eyes on her home—with its stately columns, ornate details, and many porches, set amid trees and rolling land—my mind would be overcome with a special kind of imaginative joy.

Although the house speaks to you from outside, what is truly overwhelming is the love and wonder that exist within its walls. As we would park our car on the gravel driveway, Bunny would come out to welcome us with big hugs. I always had the sense that she was just as excited as we were. The only hiccup in this poetic journey from Boston to Falls Village, over the river and through the woods in the far northwest corner of Connecticut, was that, as Aunt Bunny reminds me all the time, I would not let her kiss me goodbye.

The first thing I liked to do when I got to Bunny's was to meander through the house from room to room. I felt like I was revisiting old friends in each space. From as young as I can remember, I have lost myself in Bunny's bookshelves, especially the one at the far end of the library. I would perch on the arm of the sofa, looking at all the titles, committing the various colors of the spines to memory. I can still see certain sequences in my mind now. The house was full of spaces like this, where the imagination could wander. Every window was a glimpse of beauty, every doorway a threshold into a new space.

I remember carefully coming down the steep back stairs into the kitchen, where my Grandaddy Jimps would be the first one up, drinking coffee in his robe. I loved these times with Jimps and remember his warmth and easygoing sense of humor. The kitchen was a vibrant place when family was in Falls Village, always buzzing with energy. Eggs and bacon would fly off the stove, over the massive wooden kitchen island, and onto the table as plans would be made for the day.

Over the course of the year, the house took on distinct characters, each season activating different senses. In the summer, the screened porch would have its own smell and textures, a combination of wicker, flowers, and open air. The tones of the surroundings, complemented by the arrangement of the furniture, seemed to celebrate the gathering of family and friends as much as the beauty of the season. From the library on Christmas Eve in front of a roaring fire to the front living room before sitting down for dinner, every room in the house had its magic.

Bunny's transformation of the old barn into its current form was the first time that I remember truly marveling at her creative talent. I was always aware that something special was going on in Falls Village, but to see a dusty old barn morph into the grandest sitting room one could ever imagine—with an attached conservatory, a kitchen, and an upstairs guest room—really moved me. It was not only my Aunt Bunny's creative vision, but also her ability to realize it, whether a new barn, a vegetable garden, and greenhouse; the woodland garden; the pinecone-adorned classical pool house; or, most recently, the studio at the top of the hill. Just like the far end of the library sofa, every one of these spaces invites you to sit down, pause, and take in the beauty that surrounds you and the people with whom you are sharing that moment.

When Kate and I were considering where to get married, we both thought about Falls Village. We looked at each other, and we knew. The notion that our closest family and friends could experience the beauty and magic that my Aunt Bunny sprinkles throughout her world was incredibly meaningful for us. As we thought about how the wedding might unfold, we began to imagine the flow of our guests from the ceremony in the pool house, down through the woodlands, to a reception in the little clearing behind the conservatory. There was a sense of a formal procession uphill from the greenhouse and then a meandering waltz through the trees downhill toward the barn. As for the main reception, with dinner and dancing in a kaleidoscopic circular tent on the lawn off the library, that was a true Bunny Williams creative tour de force.

As our daughters became old enough to love making things, Bunny turned over a new leaf and spearheaded some mask-making events, the most memorable of which had a woodland theme. Acorns, leaves, branches, berries, and other natural materials all found their way into each artist's creation. My dad diligently created an amazing Bigfoot-like face with tree bark, and it prompted us to run around the woods and jump off rocks like crazed druids. As I took pictures, which I often do on visits to Aunt Bunny's, I thought that nothing could be more fitting for this magical place than our family of Bigfoots and druids frolicking in the woods.

During the winter, the warmth of Bunny's home welcomes you to find a cozy spot to sit and read or chat with family. A fire often burns in every room. After the abundance and the natural beauty of summer, Christmastime presents its own array of hues and sensations. If there is snow, the bones of the gardens are highlighted in white. Monochrome displays of contour and texture emerge amidst the hedges and ground cover. Walking from the house to the barn is slower and louder, with the snow crunching beneath your feet.

Christmas in Falls Village has been a consistent thread throughout my life. I vividly remember the excitement as we neared the house, knowing we would be greeted at the back door by my beloved Aunt Bunny. It didn't take long for me to start my traditional exploration of the house, which always culminated in my arrival at the Christmas tree in the front living room. Every year, the tree seemed bigger than the last one, and so brilliantly decorated that I could do nothing but sit still in its presence. To this day, I remain in awe of the majesty of Bunny's trees. They are otherworldly in their size and density, as much a part of the Christmas tradition as anything else.

On Christmas mornings a generation later, my daughters, Mika and Anna, would run to the hearth in the barn to see if Santa Claus had filled their stockings. They were never disappointed, and soon the rest of our family would file into the warm, firelit room to spend the morning together opening presents beneath the beautiful tree. The magic of these Christmas mornings was not lost on our daughters, and you could see the joy on their faces, surrounded by family and enthralled by a new book or toy.

In the afternoon, as the sun would sneak into the conservatory off the barn, Mika and Anna would find their way into that ethereal sanctuary full of plants and walls of glass to admire the nativity scene set up on a table facing the garden, their imaginations ignited by the elaborate clay figures. The crèche was always nestled in a cascading backdrop of moss and greenery that brought it to life. Each figure had its own story, made by an artisan long ago, and a journey that led into the hands and home of my Aunt Bunny, where every year they would be displayed with care and love, to inspire the imagination of everyone who entered the room.

As the short but energized day wound down, it would be time for Christmas dinner. There was always that moment when you would pass through the dining room and suddenly the table was brilliantly set and the fireplace aglow. That was the cue for everyone to put on their Christmas dinner attire. As a kid this was when I grew to love wearing a coat and tie like my Grandaddy Jimps or a bow tie like my dad—there was a formality to Bunny's Christmas dinners that made them even more memorable. Around the table, the mood was always light, warm, and often funny. With rare exception, every time I have eaten Christmas dinner in the dining room at Falls Village, Bunny has seated me to her left. This always made me feel deeply loved, like I was sitting in a place of honor, next to my aunt who created one beautiful scene after another for her family to enjoy. Dogs circling the table looking for crumbs and kids on their best behavior, exhausted from Christmas Day but sticking it out until dessert—these memories form a continual stream of images in my mind as long as any other thread of my life.

LIFE IN THE GARDEN

Garden paths are a wonderful way to add detail and lead visitors from one area to another. A large stone urn draws you down this diamond gravel path, which leads across the lawn to another path between the curved yew hedges.

A large fiberglass urn filled with flowers and shrubs adds exciting scale to the high-ceilinged barn living room. RIGHT: In the birdhouse village, a curved bench and twig chairs create a quiet sitting area for enjoying the scenery.

Aechmea mulfordii 'Malva' is placed in an enormous stone urn at the top of the steps leading you to the woodland garden. BELOW: Espalier apple trees are trained on the antique picket fence that surrounds the vegetable garden.

At the pool house with the Gillispie family—my niece Sarah and her husband, James, their son, Benjamin, and their wonderful dog, Franklin.

The koi pond is flanked by a boxwood hedge with
tall arborvitae columns in each corner.
Water lilies and papyrus give shade to the fish.

A faux bois bench makes a perfect place to sit and relax in the
woodland garden. RIGHT: The new sitting bedrooms always have
branches and plants from the garden. Paintings are stacked to
punctuate the height of the eighteen-foot ceilings.

A large *Disocactus phyllanthoides* "pink orchid cactus" hangs from the rafters in the greenhouse. RIGHT: A large branch placed in a tall glass vase adds drama to the studio.

A basket of cloven blossom, picked by my niece Sarah Gillispie and photographed by her husband, James, is the image I chose for the cover of the book.

Robert Reimer and I cutting flowers in the vegetable and cutting garden.

Currants are trained along the garden fence.
The only problem is that the birds often get to
the ripe berries before we do.

My nephew, Carter Blackwell, and his wife, Kate, stroll with their
wedding guests through the woodland garden to the reception.

An open door to the greenhouse, where the
collection of plants fills the tables and shelves.

The accent topiaries I planted thirty-five years ago punctuate the architecture of the house. LEFT: A detail of a table setting—creating it felt like I was arranging a still life for Matisse to paint.

A gate, paths, and steps lure the visitor from one garden to another.

The blooming dogwoods frame the
man-made woodland pond.
RIGHT: The interior of the basket house.

Light coming through the texture of the plants in the sunken garden.
A large-leaf ornamental Tropicanna ® Canna lily adds drama.

John feeding Annabelle, Bebe, and the fish.

By moving the 18th-century potting shed (now the basket house), we were able to create a special small courtyard off the vegetable garden. LEFT: A little place to sit in the sunken garden, perfect for enjoying the flowers and bees on a late afternoon.

One of my favorite tablecloths from Boxwood Linen in Chatham, New York, sets the color scheme for this dining table on the conservatory. The flowers are arranged between Christopher Spitzmiller bisque gourds.

RESOURCES

Trade Secrets
www.tradesecretsct.com
PO Box 717, Lakeville, CT 06039
(860) 364-1080
info@Project-SAGE.org
Project Sage: project-sage.org

Over the years, I have bought some of my most wonderful plants and objects from the best horticulturists, specialty nurseries, and antique dealers specializing in garden furniture and accessories from Trade Secrets, an event we created in 2002 to benefit Project Sage (women's support services). The event takes place at Lime Rock Park Racetrack in Lakeville, Connecticut, the last weekend in May. I cannot recommend it enough to those who can drive there as shipping of plants is not available.

GARDEN ORNAMENTS

Barbara Israel Garden Antiques
www.bi-gardenantiques.com
21 E 79th St., 11th Fl., New York, NY 10075
(212) 744-6281
eva@bi-gardenantiques.com
sylvia@bi-gardenantiques.com

RT Facts Design & Antiques
www.rtfacts.com
8 Old Barn Rd., Kent, CT 06757
(860) 927-1700
rtfacts@rtfacts.com

Michael Trapp Inc
michaeltrapp.com
7 River Rd., West Cornwall, CT 06796
(860) 672-6098
office@michaeltrapp.com

Withington & Company
Instagram: @WithingtonAntiques
2 Old County Rd., Cape Neck, ME 03902
(603) 498-4778
withingtonandcompany@yahoo.com

Authentic Provence
authenticprovence.com
6100 Georgia Ave., West Palm Beach, FL 33405
(561) 805-9995
info@authenticprovence.com

100 Main
https://100mainst.com/
100 Main St., Falls Village, CT 06031
(860) 453-4356
info@100mainst.com

Antiques & Artisans Village
www.antiquesandartisansvillage.com
619 Old Trolley Rd., Summerville, SC 29485
(843) 900-5386
Antiqueandartisansvillage@gmail.com

Finnegan Gallery
www.finnegangallery.com
Appointment only: 5555 North Lynch Ave., Chicago, IL 60630
(312) 738-9747
finnegangallery@sbcglobal.net

PLANTS

Plant Delights Nursery – Perennials
Plantdelights.com
9241 Sauls Rd., Raleigh, NC 27603
(919)772-4794
Plant.info@plantdelights.com

Hillside Nursery – Specialty perennials
hillsidenursery.biz
4 Norman Rd., Ashfied, MA 01330
(413) 489-1616
info@hillsidenursery.biz

Van Engelen Inc – Bulbs
www.vanengelen.com
23 Tulip Dr., PO Box 638, Bantam, CT 06750
(860) 567-8734
customerservice@vanengelen.com

New Moon Nursery – Native plugs
www.newmoonnursery.com
910 Kings Hwy., Woodstown, NJ 08098
(888) 998-1951
info@newmoonnursery.com

North Creek Nursery – Native and non-native plugs
Plant Pickup & Shipping: 124 Wedgewood Rd.,
Oxford, PA 19363
Corporate Office: 388 North Creek Rd.,
Landenberg, PA 19350
(610) 255-0100
info@northcreeknurseries.com

White Flower Farm – Perennials and shrubs
www.whiteflowerfarm.com
167 Litchfield Rd. (Route 63), Morris, CT 06763
(860) 567-8789
store@whiteflowerfarm.com

Bluestone Perennials – Perennials
www.bluestoneperennials.com
7211 Middle Ridge Rd., Madison, OH 44057
(800)852-5243
service@bluestoneperennials.com

Bluebird Nursery – Perennials
www.bluebirdnursery.com
519 Bryan St., Clarkson, NE 68629
(800)356-9164
sales@bluebirdnursery.com

Sunshine Farm & Gardens –
Native and specialty perennials
sunfarm.com
696 Glicks Rd., Renick, WV 24966
(304) 497-2208
barry@sunfarm.com

American Meadows – Bulbs and seeds
www.americanmeadows.com
2438 Shelburne Rd., Shelburne, VT 05482
(877) 309-7333
helpdesk@americanmeadows.com

Floret Flower Farm – Seeds
www.floretflowers.com
PO Box 281, Mount Vernon, WA 98273
(646) 343-4501
support@floretflowers.com

Principal photography by Annie Schlechter

Additional photography by:

Carter Berg: verso of front flyleaf and pages 20-21, 24-25, 46, 95, 101 (center left, bottom left), 102-103, 138, 144-145, 181 (top left), 214, 227, 236, 255 (bottom right & center left), 256, 258-259, 260-261, 291, 298, 310-311, 321, 326-327, 334-335, 342-343, 346-347

James Gillispie: cover, back endpaper, and pages 12, 26, 30, 40, 53 (top left, center left, bottom right), 69, 76, 100 (all), 101 (top left, top right, bottom right), 117 (top right, bottom right), 142, 181 (bottom left), 198 (center right), 199 (bottom left, top right, center right, bottom right), 254 (top left, top right, center left, center right, bottom right), 255 (top left, bottom left, top right, center right), 276-277, 302 (top right, bottom left), 303 (bottom left, bottom right), 336, 386, 391, 401 (bottom left)

Scott Groller: 4-5, 14-15, 62-63, 114-115, 150-151, 202-203, 208, 219, 263, 285, 286-287, 292-293, 333, 402 (bottom left)

John Gruen: pages 38, 75, 88, 178

First published in the United States of America in 2024 by Rizzoli International Publications, Inc.
300 Park Avenue South
New York, New York 10010
www.rizzoliusa.com

Publisher: Charles Miers
Editors: Ilaria Fusina
Production manager: Kaija Markoe
Design coordinator: Olivia Russin
Copyeditor: Claudia Bauer
Proofreader: Sarah Stump
Managing editor: Lynn Scrabis

Design by Doug Turshen with Steve Turner

ISBN: 9780847899692
Library of Congress Control Number: 2023938232
2024 2025 2026 2027 2028 / 10 9 8 7 6 5 4 3 2 1

Printed in Hong Kong